ECONOMIC EVOLUTION

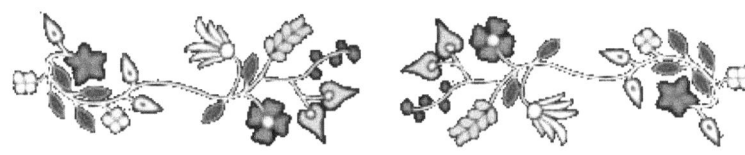

ECONOMIC EVOLUTION

Curtis W. DeCora

5 Pillars of Sustainable Economic Development

ECONOMIC EVOLUTION

Copyright © 2018 Curtis DeCora
All rights reserved.

ISBN-13: 978-1729575024
ISBN-10: 1729575021

Superior Marketing
PO Box 794
Hayward Wisconsin 54843
www.HaywardMarketing.us

Superior Marketing is a Native American owned Digital Marketing firm specializing in lead generation and outsourced sales solutions. Superior Marketing is a dba and registered and licensed in the state of Wisconsin.

Printed in the United States
First Edition: October 2018
Book cover design by Darren Landren

ECONOMIC EVOLUTION

ECONOMIC EVOLUTION

DEDICATION

I would like to dedicate this book to a couple of people.

First, my late grandfather, John Bluesky. He was my father figure and showed me the importance of hard work, dedication and commitment. You are gone, but never forgotten.

Second, my children, Kendal and Adel. Daddy loves you and appreciates putting up with my crazy business ideas and many sales meetings throughout the backwoods of Wisconsin and Minnesota.

Lastly, my grandmother, Myrna DeNasha. You've been supportive and helpful for just about everything in my life since I was a child. For that, I appreciate everything you have done.

My colleagues, associates and business partners, you have been pivotal in the growth and development of my 'self' over the last 10 years and I do appreciate your support and will continue to do what I can to support your endeavors.

ECONOMIC EVOLUTION

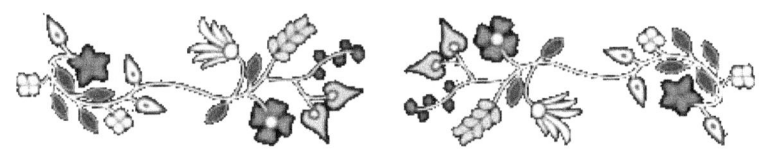

ECONOMIC EVOLUTION

ABOUT THE AUTHOR

Curtis DeCora is a Native American entrepreneur from the Lac Courte Oreilles Band of Lake Superior Chippewa in Hayward Wisconsin.

After attending Northland College (Ashland Wisconsin) studying business administration while playing collegiate level basketball, Curtis launched into the entrepreneurial octagon in 2009. After 8 years of government contracts, and workforce development sub-contracts, Curtis wanted to focus on small to medium sized business and economic development in tribal communities.

Here, in 2018, Superior Marketing has now served over 163 businesses in 4 countries, and trained 63 sales people throughout the world to become more proficient and productive sales people for their own business and employer.

The primary focus with Superior Marketing is to enhance tribal communities from an economic development standpoint. The primary motivators include job creation, economic sustainability, and diversifying the economic profile for less government dependency.

ECONOMIC EVOLUTION

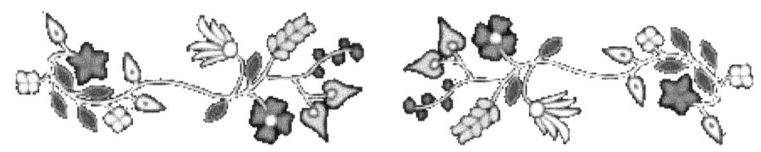

ECONOMIC EVOLUTION

TABLE OF CONTENTS

INTRODUCTION	12
STRUCTURAL EQUILIBRIUM	18
GOVERNMENT-LED	24
COMMUNITY-LED	39
TECHNOLOGY-LED	48
EDUCATION-LED	67
ENTREPRENEUR-LED	77
5 PILLARS	89
PILLAR 1: RELIABLE DATA	106
PILLAR 2: RELEVANT EDUCATION	120
PILLAR 3: REAL OPPORTUNITY	130
PILLAR 4: MOBILE TECHNOLOGY	143
PILLAR 5: YOUTH ENGAGEMENT	156
EMPOWER. DEVELOP. PROSPER	169
CONCLUSION	179

ECONOMIC EVOLUTION

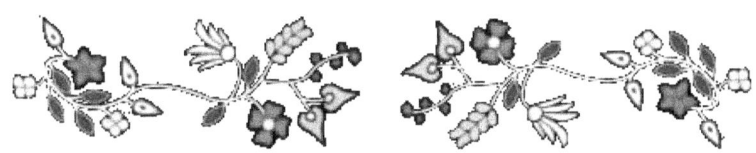

ECONOMIC EVOLUTION

CHAPTER 1
INTRODUCTION

ECONOMIC EVOLUTION

ECONOMIC EVOLUTION

INTRODUCTION

For most communities, cities, and rural areas, economic development is a factor which determines the direction of your community and, in some cases, the future of your community.

In most cases, we as humans determine where we work, live, and play based on how economically stressed an area may be, or become.

As we look into specific areas experiencing an economic boom, we usually see residual benefits of better schools, better jobs, better pay, better recreation, and better neighborhoods; among other major advantages associated with economically sounds communities.

These communities all have 5 things in common, I will call these, "5 Pillars", if you will.

ECONOMIC EVOLUTION

These 5 pillars help us gain a clearer understanding of the needs within our communities and how we can leverage them to build our very own economies from the inside-out. That's right. We build our very own communities from the inside-out.

We aren't focused in relying on a factory, manufacturing facility or corporate monsters to walk into our community because we offered them a tax-free enterprise over the next 5 years.

We are focused on leveraging the resources we have within our communities, and it all begins with people. People have capacity, people have potential, and people have ambition.

ECONOMIC EVOLUTION

Once we can identify what kind of people are within our communities, we can dive into the various forms of economic development which best suits our communities.

In some communities, it is best to utilize Community-Led Economic Development. In some communities, it is best to utilize Technology-Led Economic Development. In some communities, it is best to utilize Entrepreneurial-Led Economic Development. In some communities, it is best to utilize Educational-Led Economic Development. In other communities, it is best to ride the old wave of Government-Led Economic Development.

Over the course of the next few pages and chapters, we'll be diving into each form of economic development, why they are important and in which scenarios they are best suited to develop our very own communities, again, from the inside-out.

ECONOMIC EVOLUTION

Let's take a look into the 5 Pillars of Sustainable Economic Development, and How We Can Get Involved.

ECONOMIC EVOLUTION

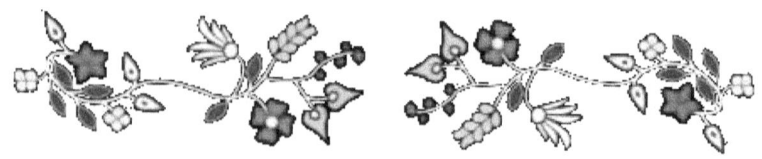

CHAPTER 2

STRUCTURAL EQUILIBRIUM

ECONOMIC EVOLUTION

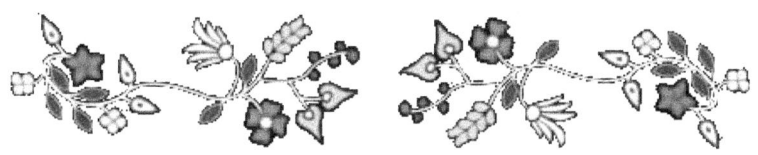

ECONOMIC EVOLUTION

STRUCTURAL EQUILIBRIUM

What is Structural Equilibrium?

Let me give you an example, then, expound upon the example by sharing information in regards to economic development and how to build a sustainable strategy leveraging this equilibrium.

Consider for one moment, the roof. This could be a residential roof, a commercial roof, or a structural roof for a garage, storage unit or otherwise. Have you ever wondered how the structure of the roof works, and operates?

Let's look at a standard 20x20 garage suitable for 2 cars, in other words a 2-car garage.

ECONOMIC EVOLUTION

In calculating out the materials needed to build the roof, we have to consider the truss bridges, 3-tab shingles, felt paper, and nails. The total weight is as follows:

24 foot truss (2 foot overhang)   =   150 lbs

A 20 foot by 20 foot garage needs 17 trusses with 16 inch center.

(I hope I'm not losing you, trust me I have a point)

17 trusses x 150 lbs =   **2,550 lbs**

1 bundle of shingles (with waste) =   80 lbs

13 bundles are required for a 20x20 roof, including the waste and ends.

13 bundles x 80 lbs =   **1,040 lbs**

On average, we are looking at a structure that weighs roughly 3,600 lbs that sits over an open space.

ECONOMIC EVOLUTION

This is the classic example of structural equilibrium. The structure of the roof allows it to hold the capacity for a minimum of 3,600 lbs

This is something we should consider when looking at how local economies are structured, how they operate, and how they are developed for greater communities.

When we look at structural equilibrium from an economic development standpoint, we have to identify which elements make up that equilibrium for your community.

In this book, and the pages to come, I cover 5 Pillars which determine the make up of a strong structural equilibrium for local economic development which are both sustainable and evolutionary.

Those pillars we are going to discuss, include:

ECONOMIC EVOLUTION

- Reliable Data
- Relevant Education
- Real Opportunity / Entrepreneurship
- Mobile Technology
- Youth Development

These topics will go into a high level of detail and granular conversational topics to help drive home the point. Let's continue on.

ECONOMIC EVOLUTION

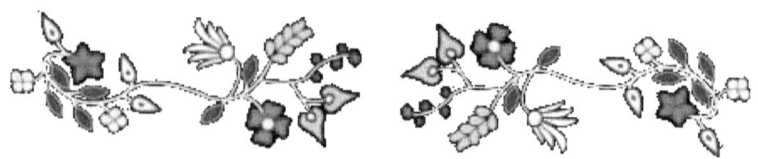

ECONOMIC EVOLUTION

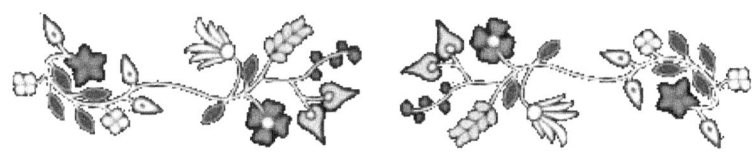

CHAPTER 3
GOVERNMENT LED ECONOMIC DEVELOPMENT

ECONOMIC EVOLUTION

GOVERNMENT-LED

What is Government-Led Economic Development?

This isn't a stance on capitalism or socialism, rather an in-depth analysis on the role government plays within our local community landscapes and how we can get involved to help drive the growth and sustainability of our communities.

Let's look at the two topics for a second, again, this isn't a stance, but rather an analysis on how they are interwoven into our local economies.

Take a look at these elements and take a look at your local economy, be it township, city, or municipality.

ECONOMIC EVOLUTION

I am more than certain you can identify which aspects your local government is practicing to ensure growth and sustainability is concerned for your local government.

Again, this is not a political stance, just an analysis.

Capitalism

Just as a recap on the role capitalism plays in our local government-led economic model.

1. <u>Ownership:</u> Assets owned by private firms
2. <u>Equality: Income determined by market</u> forces
3. <u>Prices: Prices are determined through supply and demand</u>
4. <u>Efficiency:</u> Market incentives encourage firms to cut costs
5. <u>Taxes:</u> Limited taxes, and limited government spending

ECONOMIC EVOLUTION

6. <u>Healthcare:</u> Health left to free-market

7. <u>Problems:</u> Inequality, market failure and monopolies

8. <u>Advantages:</u> Dynamic economy, initiatives for innovation and economic growth

Socialism

Let's take a look at how socialism functions with these aspects.

1. <u>Ownership:</u> Assets owned by government and cooperatives

2. <u>Equality:</u> Redistribution of income

3. <u>Price:</u> Price controls through government initiatives

4. <u>Efficiency:</u> Government owned firms have fewer incentives

5. <u>Taxes:</u> High taxes, and higher government spending

6. <u>Healthcare:</u> Healthcare provided based on government selection

7. <u>Problems:</u> Inefficient with industry, and less incentives

ECONOMIC EVOLUTION

8. <u>Advantages</u>: Promotion of equality, control of market destiny

Now that we took a quick look and analysis at both forms of economic structures, we will dive into the Government-Led economic model, while we have a clearer picture of how these initiatives are developed.

Government-Led Initiatives

Business Retention and Expansion

In most communities, this is the low hanging fruit. These particular businesses are already established, and contributing to the community in the form of job creation, revenue and taxes.

ECONOMIC EVOLUTION

A sound Business Retention and Expansion program can help improve upon revenue, expand employment and mitigate risk of loss through incentives, access to capital, and localized training programs.

The most common approach to Business Retention and Expansion are "Business Improvement Districts" or BIDs.

The participating businesses in the BID or Business Improvement District work in conjunction with the local government, pay an annual fee, or incorporate an added tax to pay for additional services to support their ventures, such as; technical assistance, procurement and contracting policies favoring local businesses, improvements to infrastructure, and implementation of training programs for workforce development.

ECONOMIC EVOLUTION

In addition to these benefits, you gain access to tertiary services, such as; marketing and promotions, street and sidewalk improvements, recruitment of complementary business, and special events.

If you're reading this and are from a small town, this sounds like the role of a Chamber of Commerce. Unfortunately, I haven't encountered a Chamber of Commerce which benefits its local enterprises off the main street.

Accelerators and Incubators

Business Accelerators and Incubators are summarized as a group of businesses that locate together in a specific area, rural, city, town, city or municipality, to gain benefits from each of their customer bases.

These baseline benefits include ease of access to other businesses in the area, think strip malls.

ECONOMIC EVOLUTION

Another form of Accelerator is a "Cluster" which include various businesses within the same industry, reaping the benefits from one another, leveraging the skill sets and workforce of one another for the pure and shared common benefits of growth and expansion.

The primary motivator, here, is innovation and productivity. Think, Silicon Valley.

In a smaller town, a business park or industrial park zoned for commercial, industrial or residential capacity are popping up in greater numbers throughout the United States.

This is the driving factor behind the "Work. Live. Play" marketing campaigns most small towns and cities are promoting.

ECONOMIC EVOLUTION

Their aim is to bring people to their communities to work in their companies spend their earrings with local businesses, and invest in the local housing and real estate market.

Value Chains

Value chains are considered the complete solution from an operational standpoint.

Your community can provide the design, production, processing, manufacturing, distribution, manufacturing, sales, and services through a variety of local businesses and entrepreneurial supply chains.

From a local economic development standpoint, this is where most Government-Led economic models fall short.

ECONOMIC EVOLUTION

While it is great to bring in an Amazon, Google, Facebook, Cargill, Rockwell Automation, Harley Davidson, and so on - the motivating factor of moving to these locations are -- tax incentives.

FUN FACT ABOUT TAX INCENTIVES

Tax free zones; including zero property tax, zero corporate tax, zero business tax, and zero income tax.

No, really. The group, SUNY (Startup New York), which is an initiative to inspire businesses to start, expand or relocate to New York state. This initiative started in 2014.

As of the 2017 report from SUNY, there has been a total of 408 jobs created in 3 years, and $50 Million in annual marketing dollars spent to promote this program.

---

5 Pillars of Sustainable Economic Development

ECONOMIC EVOLUTION

One participant in this particular Government-Led Economic Development plan includes, Dr. Greg Galvin from Incodema3D. He goes on to state, "We went from 4 employees, on up to 30 employees, and the tax incentives allowed us to recruit and target high-quality talent." However, Dr. Galvin goes on to say the headache of bureaucratic red tape, favoritism, and politics are a huge downside of this program.

Workforce Development

Local governments provide incentives and fund various programs focused on the training, development and placement of "work-ready" classified individuals into the workforce.

ECONOMIC EVOLUTION

As a byproduct of these programs, employers can garner tax credits, incentives, and in some cases free labor at the expense of the local government.

While these programs mean well, they are heavily abused, and it isn't too difficult to find loopholes.

As an example, Company A can register for these particular programs, supply the government agency with a subset of skills entry-level employees should possess prior to joining their company.

Over the course of six (6) to eight (8) weeks, Company A obtains unpaid labor, and at the end of this program, the next steps are in the hands of Company A.

ECONOMIC EVOLUTION

Company A can claim the worker isn't competent enough to place on the payroll and hire within the organization.

The governmental agency sends one or more individuals to Company A, over the course of six (6) to eight (8) weeks, Company A reaps the benefits of unpaid labor.

At the end of this cycle, again, Company A claims incompetence, or other factors deriving from an unfit employment candidate.

The end result, local businesses reap the benefits of unpaid labor. The governmental agencies are funding employment for individuals during a short period of time.

ECONOMIC EVOLUTION

The participants get the short end of the stick. They have a resume loaded with six (6) to eight (8) week stints of short-term employment - which are undesirable for most employers in today's workforce.

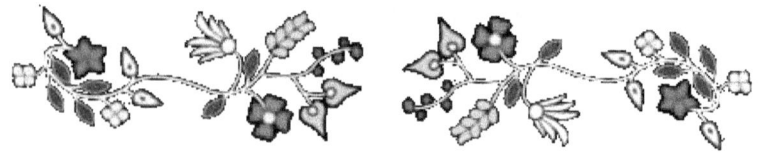

ECONOMIC EVOLUTION

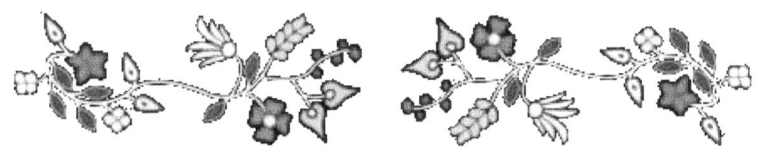

CHAPTER 4
COMMUNITY LED ECONOMIC DEVELOPMENT

ECONOMIC EVOLUTION

ECONOMIC EVOLUTION

COMMUNITY-LED

What is Community-Led Economic Development

"Community-led Development (CLD) is the process of working together to create and achieve locally owned visions and goals. It is a planning and development approach that's based on a set of core principles that (at a minimum) set vision and priorities by the people who live in that geographic community, put local voices in the lead, build on local strengths (rather than focus on problems), collaborate across sectors, is intentional and adaptable, and works to achieve systemic change rather than short-term projects."

Source:

http://inspiringcommunities.org.nz/resources/about-cld/principles

ECONOMIC EVOLUTION

The focus on Community-Led Economic Development is to identify individuals with common goals and interest, organize them and allow them to develop local initiatives that service the needs of the community.

Example: Re:Vision (Denver, Colorado)

This example is one that best exemplifies Native American communities. The founder, Eric Kornacki, began in organization in Denver, Colorado, specifically the Westwood neighborhood.

Eric's story describes a community with failing schools, businesses were leaving, high poverty ratings, no grocery stores, along with a wide range of challenges from personal health, housing, and economic struggles.

ECONOMIC EVOLUTION

Re:Vision began their Community-Led Economic Development initiative with food. That's right. Food.

The organization began a community-led agriculture program. They realized that food has the power of bringing people together, from grandma's home cooking, or a potluck dinner.

The primary goal was to help residents of Westwood grow their own food through this agriculture program. The residents were turning their yards into gardens full of fresh fruits and vegetables. This program was called, "Back Yard Gardens."

Other phases of the total development included, Promotoras, which were trained local residents employed to help their neighbors and friends grow back yard gardens. This "Pay-it-forward" model creates a sense of ownership in the community.

ECONOMIC EVOLUTION

Other additions included, Feed Westwood, which is a community-owned food system provided to low-income families through vouchers, Supplemental Nutrition Assistance Program (SNAP) and Food Stamp programs. These dollars are now staying within the neighborhood, in the amount of $13 Million dollars on an annual basis.

La Cocina is a Community-Led Nutrition and Cooking Education program to help streamline the products from backyard gardens and Feed Westwood to help families cook homemade nutritious meals for families to help battle the onset challenges of obesity and poor nutrition.

Lastly, this Community-Led Economic Development initiative produced a food co-op. The Westwood Food Coop is a member-owned and operated grocery store providing jobs, training programs, increased health and more importantly capacity building.

ECONOMIC EVOLUTION

The residual benefits of a Community-Led Economic Development model includes resource ownership, capacity building, and increases in wealth and localized community-owned assets.

The member-owners, employees and community members are gaining invaluable skills from business ownership, management, financial management, facilities maintenance, gardening, production, packaging, distribution, marketing and the list goes on.

The Westwood Food Cooperative keeps profits in the community. This is a form of community wealth building - an approach to building wealth that is locally owned and locally controlled.

We believe this is a powerful model for change.

ECONOMIC EVOLUTION

"Through the Westwood Food Cooperative, Re:Vision is showing what Community-Led economic models should look like. This is a business that exists to serve the specific needs of the community, and therefore can never be uprooted or outsourced somewhere else." - Denver Mayor, Michael Hancock.

This is a great Community-Led economic model which empowers the members of the community, develops capacity and skill sets, while providing a pathway to prosperous and generous qualifies of life.

ECONOMIC EVOLUTION

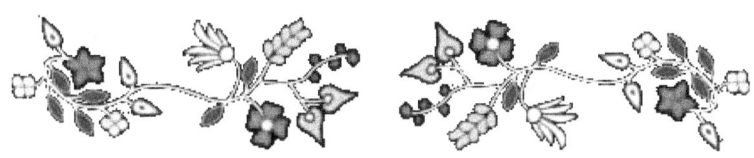

ECONOMIC EVOLUTION

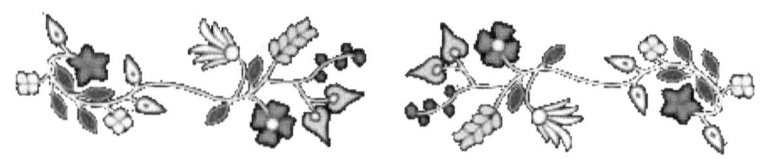

CHAPTER 5
TECHNOLOGY LED ECONOMIC DEVELOPMENT

ECONOMIC EVOLUTION

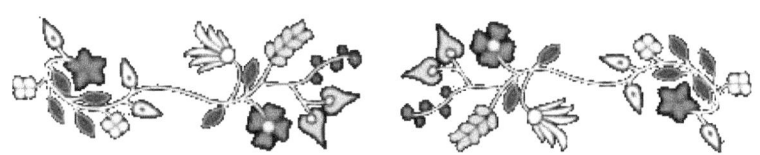

ECONOMIC EVOLUTION

TECHNOLOGY-LED

What is Technology-Led Economic Development?

Technology-Led Economic Development is based on the notion that the future of innovation revolve around both knowledge and technology Therefore, develop the capacity of those within our community through technology based platforms, while learning the intricacies of high-demand technology based employment.

Workforce Development

The first element in tech-led economic models includes assessing the current workforce that is present, establishing a baseline of knowledge and developing programs, training and pathways for career advancement based on those baseline metrics.

ECONOMIC EVOLUTION

While basic levels of literacy are required, the most coveted employees in the workforce require specialized skills, and relevant training.

Some economists consider today's market the "Knowledge Economy."

We will talk more about the educational aspect in the "Education-Led Economic Development" chapter. I wanted to simply touch upon the importance of technology and innovation pertaining to education and human capital development.

Research and Development

When we hear the term, "Research and Development" we typically think about Wayne Enterprises, and Lucius Fox putting together some of these amazing base jumping, and light-weight clothing items allowing Bruce to

ECONOMIC EVOLUTION

engage in underground vigilante activities to save the world from super villains.

However, every business must undergo a phase of research to ensure they have the sound and reliable data to make informed decision about a business venture, investment, acquisition, merger or necessity to expand your workforce.

All of the aforementioned require extension research.
Tech-led initiatives drive innovations for new products, new services, new processes, and new ways to conduct business in the digital world.

Consider for one moment, mobile applications.

Yes, you have mobile applications of varying status; native applications, hybrid applications and web applications.

ECONOMIC EVOLUTION

They all provide the same deliverables, however, differ greatly from development, intellectual property, data, and valuation of your model once fully developed.

The point is, mobile applications, dramatically changed how we live our lives. Gone are the days of going to Sears, JC Penney, and the local auto dealership and relying on the salesperson to provide you with the accurate information on the product to meet your needs.

Mobile applications have enabled us to search the entire city, state, region or country for pricing on the product, services or solution you're seeking.

This has allowed anyone providing products, services or solutions to enter into the global economy, and monetize on customers not just in your town, city, or state, but all over the world.

ECONOMIC EVOLUTION

Tech-led Economic Development is about driving innovation to create economic growth on a local level through the distribution of value-centric solutions into a commercial space for monetization.

You can take a product, service, or solution, leverage technology, innovate your local economic profile.

The beauty about research and development, is that you can utilize it anywhere for any industry.

Let's take our local energy source.

Most of us are using various forms of energy to power of city, towns, homes, and devices.

ECONOMIC EVOLUTION

Solar power is an industry most communities have no tapped into, hydroelectric power, and wind power.

Whether your community focuses on manufacturing, production, distribution, farming, marketing, education, healthcare, or governmental services - all of these industries can be innovated through technology.

Remote and Virtual Business Processes

One of the biggest and most noticeable industries making waves right now - remote and virtual work.

In 2017, I was an entrepreneur with a capacity of 6 clients for digital marketing and lead generation.

I was working close to 78-80 hours a week, spending most of my time up during the wee hours of the night focusing on finalizing the deliverables

ECONOMIC EVOLUTION

for clients, while preparing my call sheets, and outreach activities for the next day for the same batch of clients.

I was driving myself into the ground, sleeping close to 3 hours a day, pounding pots of coffee just to keep productive and awake.

In April of 2017, I found someone who was a "Virtual Assistant" and they were asking me to send them work.

The language barrier made it difficult to understand their intent, rather than their request.

After a couple of very long conversations so I could best gain a handle on what they were capable of handling as far as outsourced tasks. We discussed everything from the standard data entry, down to Managed LinkedIn, and cold calling campaigns. Some were highly proficient in

ECONOMIC EVOLUTION

email campaigns. The VAs were highly proficient in writing sales copy, some were very good with researching article topics, and were able to help me develop mounds upon mounds of content for our SEO strategies with my clients.

After 5 months of shuffling Virtual Assistants from all over the world, I found a, very good, small group of Virtual Assistants from various parts of the world.

The VAs did everything from writing my articles for SEO clients, writing and sending my emails for email marketing campaigns, building out my ringless voicemail campaigns, running my text message campaigns and I could simply sit in my home office and make direct and targeted cold calls for my Lead Generation clients.

ECONOMIC EVOLUTION

I had opened up close to 60 hours a week and kept my margins high, allowing me to add on 4 more clients - turning my clients load into 10 clients. I'm now working 18-20 hours every week, and making 40% more every month, while maintaining the integrity of my deliverables and quality of services.

We eventually grew to 20 Virtual Assistants, and 30 clients paying an average of $2,000 per month in retainers and performance bonuses.

Now, I was working close to 85-90 hours a week trying to keep everyone on the same page. It was like herding cats. I encountered excuse after excuse, and it was all my fault. I wasn't setting the same strict set of guidelines and rules I once established to whittle down the best of the best into my team of highly polished Virtual Assistants committed to my goal, my mission and overall object in serving clients.

ECONOMIC EVOLUTION

I had to scale back on clients, and focus on the core of my firm. Quality. As communities and tribal organizations are concerned, there are very few reasons why disadvantaged communities aren't leveraging remote and virtual services in conjunction with utilizing and training in a local workforce form the community with which it resides.

Example 1:   Sparkki: An Online Learning Platform

Sparkki is a Salt Lake City based programming company, offering an online learning platform providing access to technology to innovate the very way enterprise level companies do business.

Sparkki took all of the things that made online learning platforms great, and put them all into one single, consolidated platform, in Sparkki.

ECONOMIC EVOLUTION

Sparkki is working with companies big and small to help innovate their processes to help with resource allocation, expediting workflow, improving upon the training and development of employees within an organization, while helping companies create additional revenue streams through one platform.

I, personally, have developed an online course for sales people who wish to develop their capacity in prospecting and filling their sales pipelines. That is the biggest challenge all sales people struggle with, developing qualified sales pipeline.

My course has helped sales people from all over the world gain a clearer understanding of how to prospect effectively with a refined and granular course offering without me, the instructor, present in any of the content delivery.

ECONOMIC EVOLUTION

This is a fully automated and pre-recorded course with built in quizzes and tests ensuring for content retention, competency skills, and activity reports they must submit via the online portal I can review and discuss with the students.

This process helps the students formulate a customized plan to help them be more productive as a sales professional, entrepreneur, or utilize as a sales manager in their sales training programs.

Through technology-led initiatives, I, personally, was able to leverage the newest forms of technology to service clients from all over the world, while creating a new revenue stream.

ECONOMIC EVOLUTION

Example 2:   **Agent Alive: The Mobile Insurance Agent**

Agent Alive is an insurance agency based out of Arlington, Texas which leverages the power of mobile applications to grow and expand their agency.

Agent Alive allows agencies from all over the United States to acquire insurance clients from anywhere in the 50 states, provided they're licensed to service those states.

This mobile application allows those seeking insurance, to connect with insurance agents via Live video chat, conduct a real-time document exchange directly through the mobile application, share screens and record discussions, make payments for policies and premiums, set up recurring payment, document scanning, e-signing capabilities, and virtual

ECONOMIC EVOLUTION

property inspections for home, auto, ATV, personal watercraft, and other insurable assets.

Agent Alive is allowing insurance agencies the chance to innovate and compete with the esurance, The General and other online insurance platforms which aggregate carriers and policies as a lead generation source and allow insurance seeking individuals and businesses to obtain insurance with a few clicks.

The challenge that exists with online platforms, is the fact that you can end up underinsured, over insured, or improperly classified for insurance categories and deductibles.

If any of those scenarios were to occur, your next challenge is to connect with a live agent who may deem liable for those insurance gaps.

ECONOMIC EVOLUTION

That's where Agent Alive comes in.

Now, you connect with a live agent that is licensed and insured to offer insights into your insurance coverage, and ensure you're properly covered without overpaying or obtaining under coverage.

As a consumer, you no longer have to sit in an insurance agents office for hours on end scanning documents, signing documents, and the worst part of sitting in traffic, or taking extra long lunch breaks from work to obtain insurance.

You can insure someone from New York while sitting in your home office while residing in California.   This is the value of technology-led economic development. Those revenues are filtered into companies and organizations, which pay employees and filter those dollars back into the local economy.

ECONOMIC EVOLUTION

Technology-Led Economic Development is all about innovating the local economy by supplying local individuals with job opportunities.

In the same sentence, we can mention the fact that management, maintenance, and further development of the marketing campaigns required to drive demand for more clients through the mobile application.

ECONOMIC EVOLUTION

ECONOMIC EVOLUTION

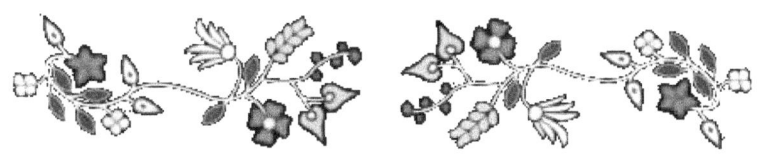

CHAPTER 6

EDUCATION LED ECONOMIC DEVELOPMENT

ECONOMIC EVOLUTION

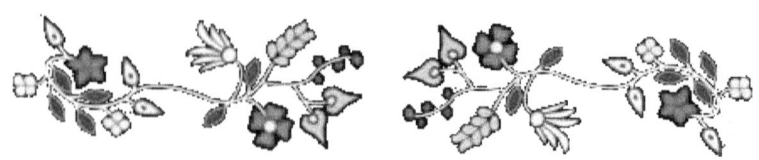

ECONOMIC EVOLUTION

EDUCATION-LED

What is Education-Led Economic Development?

This is likely the most common form of initiative you'll see in your local economy. The most common initiatives are workforce development with training and education emphasis.

This is the Education-Led Economic Development model.

The entire goal of an Education-Led Economic model is to educate and train the local workforce in areas specific to the enterprise, industry, and trends of your local community.

Some communities are heavily focused on forestry, mining, tourism, and transportation, to name a few. These particular areas work with local

ECONOMIC EVOLUTION

institutions of higher learning; such as community colleges, universities, vocational schools, apprenticeship and internship programs.

These programs are great for bridging the connect from educational institutions and programs to local employers, as they should. These programs and institutions help solve a real world challenge right in our very own communities by providing local enterprise with qualified and competent work-ready individuals trained and prepared to be productive employees.

One of the primary challenges we see with community colleges and universities, are programs geared towards personal enrichment and personal preference. While these are great for the individual's interests and exploring interests one might have. The pathway isn't ideal. These individuals aren't prepared for any of the jobs in the local community,

ECONOMIC EVOLUTION

unless they explore the path of Entrepreneurship - which we will talk about in the next chapter, Entrepreneur-Led Economic Development.

Education-Led Economic Development always starts with data. What kind of data is available from the local workforce, local employers and regional sectors employing some of the most individuals in that particular community?

Data is absolutely crucial, and the reason why we include data as one of the pillars of sustainable economic development.

Data can tell us where the gaps reside, where the demand sits, and what kind of supply we can provide to the local businesses. While our local employers and businesses are always looking for top-tier talent, we don't always get the opportunity to explore those top-tier clients due to the labor shortage in qualified and competent individuals.

ECONOMIC EVOLUTION

Let's take tribal communities, for example.

Tribal communities are constantly trying to hire administrative level employees from their very own tribes. That isn't a reality when we take into considering the amount of individuals in the community hosting those particular skill sets.

We end up hiring outside of the tribal labor pool, and everyone is upset that companies aren't hiring tribal members.

Sound familiar?

Part of the Education-Led economic model is to create progressions in educational and training pathways. Progressions built into each enterprise, business, and organization. These progressions allow proper ramp up periods in training, skill attainment and competence.

ECONOMIC EVOLUTION

When your employees are properly trained, obtain invaluable skills associated with the job at hand, the tasks to complete, and competence needed to be a productive and empowered employee. You're now following the EMPOWER. DEVELOP. PROSPER mantra of sustainable economic development.

One of the most unpopular opinions to discuss, include Tribal Government. When we think about the elected officials we vote into office every two (2) years, or four (4) years, depending on how your electoral policies are developed. We are essentially putting people into office with minimal training, experience and competence. While they're highly skilled and proficient in their previous roles, government is an entirely different kind of role.

Most tribal governments I have worked with in the past 10 years include elected officials. In most cases, the first year includes these elected

ECONOMIC EVOLUTION

officials becoming acquainted with governance. The second year include becoming familiar with the business conducted and tribal affairs. That's a two year learning curve.

There really isn't any quick and dirty answer to help bring tribal leaders up to speed on the critical matters of the tribal community, as a whole.

However, the education and training gap is something that should be a focus for most tribal communities These are large sums of dollars spent on training, travel, and workshops to help tribal leaders become skilled and competent in matters of the tribal community.

In a Community-Led economic model, members of the community participate in various groups, associations and committees related to tribal affairs. These groups become familiar with budgetary issues,

ECONOMIC EVOLUTION

procurement, human resource processes, and of course, economic development, among other areas of tribal government.

In highly skilled positions, it is very difficult to simply hire and train, due to the heavy training and ramp up period. It is very expensive, very cost ineffective, and isn't serving the best needs of the enterprise, business and organization.

ECONOMIC EVOLUTION

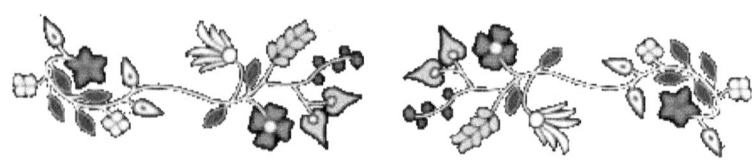

ECONOMIC EVOLUTION

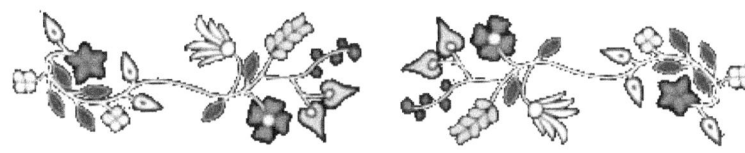

CHAPTER 7
ENTREPRENEUR LED ECONOMIC DEVELOPMENT

ECONOMIC EVOLUTION

ECONOMIC EVOLUTION

ENTREPRENEUR-LED

What is Entrepreneur-Led Economic Development?

Entrepreneur-Led Economic Development is about opportunity. We want to look at the amount of opportunity available in our communities.

When we look at the amount of money spent by our community businesses, industry, manufacturing, distribution, marketing, transportation, and other organizations in our community, we see millions of dollars. Millions of dollars going to pay for products and services to support our local businesses.

We look at everything from the toilet paper, to business cards, on up to the equipment we purchase to operate our businesses.

ECONOMIC EVOLUTION

In the retail capacity, we look at inventory, shelving, displays, employee attire, name tags, software, Point-of-Sale systems, signage, advertising, and the list goes on. Every business has overhead expenses to simply keep the doors open, they are spending large sums of money for these components.

The challenge resides with these businesses purchasing these items from the internet, typically from companies across the pond. Those dollars are leaving our community, also known as, "Capital Flight." They have a tremendous impact on our local economies.

Let's look at a quick study from a rural U.S community far from metropolitan locations, much like the tribal communities throughout the United States.

ECONOMIC EVOLUTION

Figure 1: Independent Study, National Chains vs Independent Local

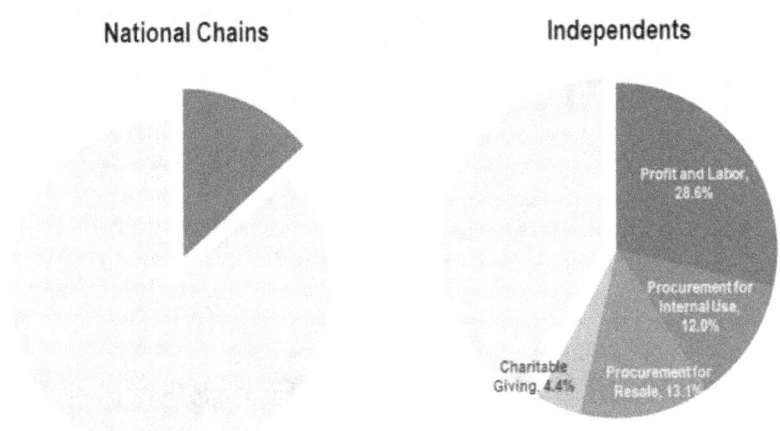

In this specific study, you can see how this may impact your local economy. If we look at every $100 spent in a business within your community. If that business is a national chain, you can expect $13.60 to stay in the community and circulate for payroll, utilities, advertising, equipment, and raw materials or inventory. Keep in mind, these items can and should be purchased from within your very own community from entrepreneurs and local enterprise.

ECONOMIC EVOLUTION

Conversely, if you were to purchase from a local business, $58.20 will stay in the community for payroll, utilities, advertising, equipment, and raw materials or inventory.

Why Buy Local

In a buy local initiative, and Entrepreneur-Led Economic Development model, our focus is on procurement for vetting out local suppliers of goods and services which meet the needs of our local restaurant/hospitality, retail, service, and industry.

The multiplier effect for a National Chain vs Local Business in this particular study indicates a 428% increase in revenue recirculation.

As members, citizens, and residents of our very own communities, we need to realize the impact a "Buy Local" initiative has on your local economy

ECONOMIC EVOLUTION

for purposes of job creation, infrastructure, and reinvestment in community improvements.

These initiatives start and end with entrepreneurs.

The Future of Economy

This is purely opinion. Over the last 36 to 40 months, I have been noticing a trend in various companies across the United States. The majority of these companies are cutting back on expenses, reducing hours, and number of employees.

Businesses really only have three options to reduce overhead expenses. They can (1) Automate, (2) Delegate, and (3) Eliminate. Those are the only options in cutting costs.

ECONOMIC EVOLUTION

Automation

In order for businesses to automate, they tend to look towards technology to solve their challenges. This includes incorporating e-commerce, mobile responsive websites to accept applications for vacant positions, databases to search inventory, special events, or other related searchable items. In some national chain restaurants, we are starting to see kiosks which take your order, and payment, while beginning your order. The employees are downsized to simply work behind the counter in the kitchen, and they have removed the smiling face at the counter to take your order and ask, "Would you like fries with that?"

Delegation

Delegation is simply defined as passing off dubious and monotonous time sucking tasks to someone else in the organization. Well, this has been

ECONOMIC EVOLUTION

transforming dramatically in the last 5 to 10 years. Now, companies from all walks of life are looking to Virtual Assistants and Remote Work. If your agency has 8 hours a week in data entry, these agencies are outsourcing those 8 hours of tasks to a foreign based individual for $3-$4 per hour.

What once cost a company 8 hours of work multiplied by the $12/hr wage, an estimated $96 + payroll liabilities, now costs a company $32, at a flat rate.

These same tasks can be just as well outsourced to a local Virtual Assistant on sub-contracted Executive Assistant. When we remain local in our outsourced and delegated tasks, those dollars recirculate to local establishments for essentials of that individual. This is something we tend to overlook as business owners. While it is beautiful and sexy to pay $32 for these tasks to be completed, we have an obligation, duty and

ECONOMIC EVOLUTION

responsibility to our communities to recirculate dollars as many times as possible.

Elimination

Another form of cutting costs is to simply remove those specific tasks, and resources deployed for those successfully completed tasks. Most companies find that by focusing on delegating tasks and automating, you're eliminating excess tasks, steps, or processes This becomes a byproduct of the first two options; automation and delegation.

Another way to eliminate tasks are to audit your current processes associated with your revenue producing activities. While we audit our processes, we typically find additional tasks proven to add limited to no effect on your revenue production activities. These are the tasks we want to eliminate.

ECONOMIC EVOLUTION

Let me give you an example.

When I was working with a company in 2016. The standardized process for daily prospecting, sales, and associated activities included numerous tasks for reporting, documenting, and tracking. The company used a customized version of SalesForce.com. If you're familiar with SalesForce.com, you'll quickly realize that you can pull hundreds upon hundreds of reports from the data entered by Account Executives, Senior Sales Executives, and so on.

In one of the weekly sales meeting with management, I asked the question. "Why are we entering data into SalesForce.com, only to send out a separate Excel spreadsheet, we have to update manually on a weekly basis?" I recommended the modification to the sales forecast dashboard which pull our critical key performance indicators (KPIs) as it relates to productivity. Productivity drives a predictable sales performance within any organization, among less skilled and more skilled sales professionals

ECONOMIC EVOLUTION

for high-performing sales teams. The dashboard was modified, and the reports were now compiled into the Sales Manager and Sales Directors monthly, weekly, daily and hour-by-hour reporting functions in SalesForce.com, and the sales team opened up four (4) hours each month, creating more productivity. After all, upper level management wanted to see higher levels of productivity; more calls, more meetings, more statements, more quotes, and contracts created in SalesForce.com.

This is an example of eliminating tasks for higher levels of productivity, efficiency, and more transparent reporting.

As you will find, more and more companies are going to become a product of the delegation and automation phases. If you take a closer look at the denser populations throughout the United States, you will find more companies focused on outsourcing tasks to companies that can fulfill or automate through software, or innovative technologies.

ECONOMIC EVOLUTION

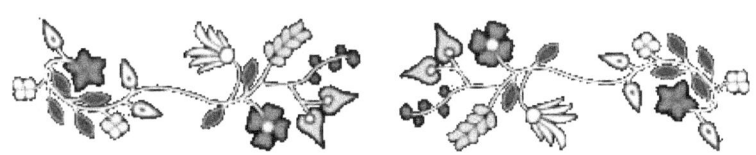

ECONOMIC EVOLUTION

CHAPTER 8

5 PILLARS OF SUSTAINABLE TRIBAL ECONOMIC DEVELOPMENT

ECONOMIC EVOLUTION

5 PILLARS

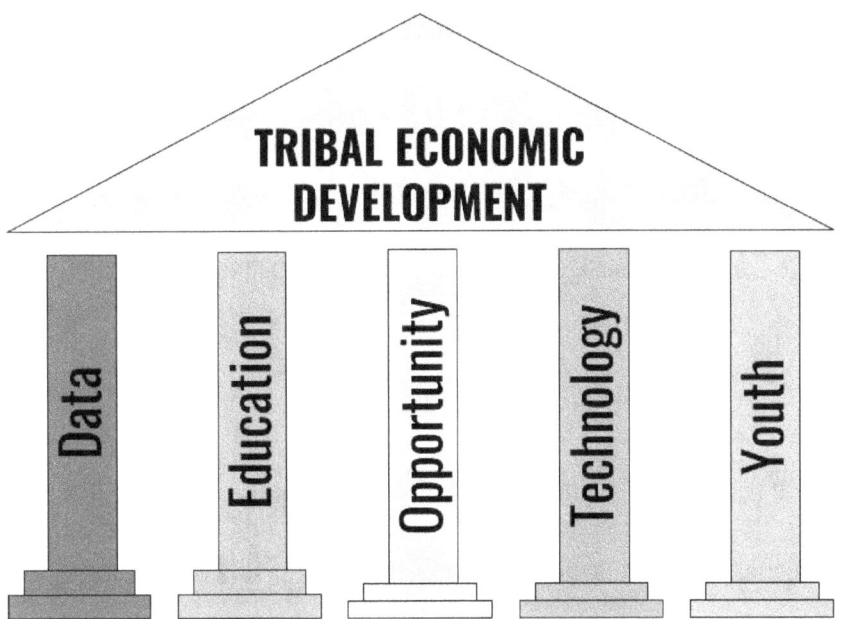

What are the 5 Pillars of Sustainable Tribal Economic Development?

There are 573 Federally Recognized tribes in the United States. When we as tribal members, community advocates and leadership constituents look to solutions best addressing the economic landscape of the tribal status,

ECONOMIC EVOLUTION

there are diverse challenges. These diverse challenges stem from a few areas, one is the geographic location. Whether the tribe is in a urban community, or rural community - the challenges are very much different.

One tribe that is located in the rural Northwoods of Wisconsin will not have the same challenges as a tribe in heavily populated metropolitan location.

What comes to mind are tribes like Lac Courte Oreilles Band of Lake Superior Chippewa, and trying to compare them to Gila River Indian Community - whereas the economic development plans for each community will be entirely different in design, resources and implementation.

The question we as tribal members, community advocates and leadership constituents ask ourselves is, "How can we participate, help or 'chip in'?"

ECONOMIC EVOLUTION

Let me be the first today, that's a great question and those are the types of people we need to reel in, foster and empower to make massive waves of contribution within our very own communities.

Without further adieu, let's dive into the 5 Pillars of Sustainable Tribal Economic Development. We have the three (3) R's, which are real, reliable, and relevant, as well as two additional surprising factors we should be considering.

Pillar 1: Reliable Data

In any type of improvement program we must measure and track before we can improve. Consider the last diet plan you started, what was the first step? You had to measure your waist, weigh yourself, and track your height and daily calorie consumption.

ECONOMIC EVOLUTION

Does that sound familiar? Of course it does!

This is also true for sustainable economic development. We must measure the revenue, expenses, resources, assets, and liabilities associated with our tribal community. Once we have a clear picture, we can design a plan with clear and concise deliverables that allow us to make improvements.

This all starts with reliable data.

Pillar 2: Relevant Education

When we look at the educational opportunities afforded to us in our tribal communities, most of us aren't blessed enough to have a tribal colleges and universities (TCU's). These institutions are great as they can provide a great career pathways incorporating school-to-work type of partnerships, whereas local tribal enterprises can obtain training,

ECONOMIC EVOLUTION

certifications and specialized degrees that provide the local tribal enterprises with a highly qualified workforce.

Unfortunately, most TCU's aren't engaged wholly with the tribal economic community. The TCU's prove 2+2 programs to bridge the students with an educational pathway to obtain an Associates degree and afford them a streamlined path to a Bachelor and Master's degree programs. These are great! This still leaves a gap with the qualified workforce.

Skilled trades and specialized programs should be created to train, certify and license local tribal members that feed directly into the tribal enterprises as it relates to the tribal economic development plan.

Let me provide an example. There are community colleges that focus on transportation or construction trades, but have no pathway to direct placement upon completion. This is the simplest and most cost effective

ECONOMIC EVOLUTION

form of recruitment, hiring, and managing as most participants likely already completed an internship or work-based-learning opportunity with these enterprises.

We are addressing the challenges of; high employee turnover, unqualified workforce, training expenses, and ramp up time to bring new hires up to speed.

A great example is the Lac Courte Oreilles Ojibwa Community College with their Early Childhood Development program, which addresses all of the certifying, practicum hours, licensing, and experience needs, as well as the cultural sensitivity training needed to ensure the new hire is experienced working with culture, language, and family or community dynamics. This program pours new graduates directly into one of four (4) early-childhood development centers in the Lac Courte Oreilles community.

ECONOMIC EVOLUTION

Pillar 3: Real Opportunity

As a Native entrepreneur, I personally see the whole landscape of sustainable tribal economic development moving the route of fostering tribal entrepreneurship. In order to provide real opportunities for tribal entrepreneurs, we must engage in business incubators and produce tribal procurement that supports and empowers tribal entrepreneurs.

We have tribal preference for our hiring practices within tribal organizations and enterprises, but rarely do we have a process or policy that states you should consider tribal entrepreneurs first priority the bid on a contract or outsourced service.

If a tribal procurement process empowering tribal entrepreneurs were available with a business incubator offering training, supports, and shared resources for all tribal entrepreneurs to succeed. This would be of

ECONOMIC EVOLUTION

massive business.

Here is an example of how this would work. As a tribal entrepreneur, I approach tribal leaders and business development corporations often in regards to proposing my products, services and solutions. My own tribe has saved tremendous amounts of money by utilizing my services and I turn around and purchase gas, eat at the restaurants, and shop at their retail locations.

The money stays in the community.

Every tribe has skilled tradesman in the areas of landscaping, carpentry, masonry, electrical, mechanics, heavy equipment operators and commercial driver's license holders - and so on. These entrepreneurs can bid on contracts with the tribal health center, casino, convenience stores, and any other asset properties the tribe owns. Again, the money stays in

ECONOMIC EVOLUTION

the community, we are supporting tribal entrepreneurs and through the incubators empowering members through capacity building, and training opportunities.

To take this a step further, the tribal organizations with 8(a) or HubZone certified enterprises can subcontract to these entrepreneurs, save massive amounts of money on payroll liabilities, insurance, and managerial oversight, while satisfying the federal requirements of minority workforce.

Pillar 4: Mobile Technology

Technology has leveled the playing field for any business, provided these businesses are leveraging the power of technology. I personally know two to three dozen digital entrepreneurs that have built 6-figure businesses from their kitchen table while leveraging the power of social media

ECONOMIC EVOLUTION

platforms. In their pajamas, they can create aggressive marketing campaigns to help businesses generate more qualified leads, quotes, and clients through free platforms like Facebook, YouTube, Google, Instagram, Snapchat, Twitter and many others.

In addition to digital entrepreneurs, mobile technology can benefit premise-based enterprises, much like we have on tribal lands, with online ordering, e-commerce and digital products. We can generate and approve loan applications from people from all over the United States we have never met, nor will we ever meet. Within 24 hours, we lend short-term loans and can generate millions in revenue through this mobile technology.

Other considerations include training and technical assistance through mobile technology. I have been involved with Community Development Financial Institutions since 2010 and realized there were some geo-based

ECONOMIC EVOLUTION

challenges associated with supporting tribal entrepreneurship. Many of the participants seeking to start a small business had to arrive at the office, take a 60 minute class in financial management, marketing, management, budgeting, and so on. The biggest challenge these participants experienced was associated with transportation, specifically in rural areas. Mobile technology can solve that. An online business training and technical assistance module can train in program participants in all areas of business ownership, while allowing the Native CDFI organization full transparency to the reporting functions of their progress. These are progress reports can be part of their development plan for the next round of funds released for the aspiring tribal entrepreneur.

Personally, I took three (3) online courses to help me develop an entirely new service which produces ⅓ of my annual revenue. These courses were $299 each and I have made that back on my first 4 clients. New client

ECONOMIC EVOLUTION

acquisition can be done from the comfort of my home, in my pajamas, updates and maintenance are completed from my laptop or mobile device. Remote services are what I'm talking about here. Mobile technology allows Remote Services to be a critical service most companies tend to hire for - they can now outsourced that to businesses like mine.

Pillar 5: Youth Engagement

This is the final pillar, only because I personally find it the most crucial component. I'm a strong advocate for youth development, specifically tribal youth development. My younger years included becoming a three sport athlete, and going on to play basketball at the collegiate level. The character developed includes aspects of leadership, team-building, self-improvement, and taking direction for the greater good of the group or team. These are characteristics most hiring managers and recruiters are looking for.

ECONOMIC EVOLUTION

This process should start early, and here is why. As a Native tribal youth continues on with their younger years and advance into high school, they begin to craft their vision for their future. There are two boats they can take post-graduation.

Boat number one includes, going off to the university of their choice, obtaining a bachelor's, master's or doctorate degree in one specialization - only to return and help improve their own community, become a leader, if you will. Boat number two includes, working in one of the local tribal enterprises, climbing the corporate ladder, and helping improve their community internally.

The internal conversation that goes on with the youth revolves around, "How can I participate, and do I want to participate?"

ECONOMIC EVOLUTION

Our job, duty and obligation as tribal members, community advocates and leadership constituents is to engage and empower our youth to participate. Early on, we should encourage them to participate in youth entrepreneurship to grow a desire for a skilled trade, profession, or pillar in the community for language or cultural preservation. Our programs and organizations should focus on creating career pathways, training opportunities, internships and apprenticeships while they're still in school.

Not only will this allow the youth of our community to begin crafting their vision of the future with our communities in mind, but how they can make an impact early and be a critical component of the economic landscape.

Where the importance of youth engagement shines the brightest, go to your General Membership meetings and listen to the topics.
Most topics include, "Why are we not hiring our own people?" The most common answer is, "We don't have any qualified members to run this

ECONOMIC EVOLUTION

enterprise." There are two boats I referenced earlier in this pillar which address this specific challenge. It is a recruitment pipeline that generates interest and engages the youth within our very own tribal enterprises, while helping them craft a vision of their future and the impact they can make on their own communities.

Sustainable Tribal Economic Development is a hot topic with just about every tribal community, and there is no one-size-fits-all solution, magic bullet, or cookie cutter template to solve these challenges. If we focus on these pillars, we have the framework to improve upon our communities with a diligent and powerful approach which ropes in every tribal member to play an active role from youth to elderly.

ECONOMIC EVOLUTION

ECONOMIC EVOLUTION

CHAPTER 9
RELIABLE DATA

ECONOMIC EVOLUTION

PILLAR 1: RELIABLE DATA

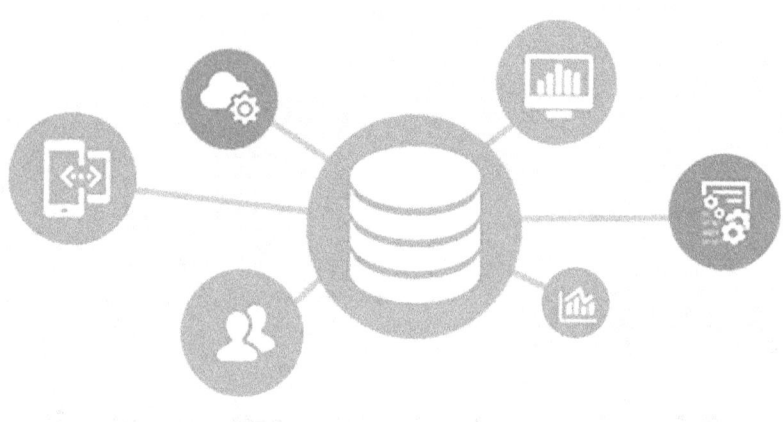

The first pillar in creating a sustainable tribal economic development plan includes, reliable data.

In order to truly create a plan that is effective, efficient and engaging, you should always start with reliable data.

ECONOMIC EVOLUTION

Consider the last time you went on a diet. Which steps did you take? Most of us weigh ourselves first, then we measure our midsections, thighs, arms, and chest, among other areas. We break down a caloric budget that would work for us, something like, "2,000 calories per day, maximum" and leverage technology like MyFitnessPal or similar apps. This is the stage of collecting reliable data. Now, that we have our data compiled and analyzed, we can begin our process.

Does that sound familiar? If not, I would be happy to help you with this. I've been a personal trainer for nearly 11 years but that's more of a hobby.

WHICH DATA IS NECESSARY

Demographics

What are demographics? Demographics are defined as statistical data

ECONOMIC EVOLUTION

relating to the population and particular groups within it. What are the demographics of your local community?

<u>Typical demographic categories include</u>:

+ Race

+ Ethnicity

+ Gender

+ Age

+ Education

+ Profession

+ Occupation

+ Income level, and

+ Marital status

This type of data can be found within your Central Data Warehouse (CDW). CDW's are databases developed to allow your programs and organizations

ECONOMIC EVOLUTION

to access sensitive data for programs, services, and grant opportunities among other areas such as health care, housing, or social programs.

Labor Data

Labor data is critical to determine the number of unemployed, underemployed, employed, and so on.

You can break down those categories into more granular topics such as:

+ Regular employees

+ Extended temporary employees

+ Temporary employees

+ Part-tIme employees

+ On-call employees

+ Administrative employees and

+ Contractual employees

ECONOMIC EVOLUTION

These categories are crucial in determining if the current workforce is engaging in gainful employment. Gainful employment refers to the employment status as it relates to steady work and payment from their current employer. Other resources indicate Gainful Employment as "Steady work and payment that covers the essentials catering to the desired quality of life within the given geographic location and qualifications."

Consumer Data

This data is gathered from the United States Census Bureau, and Department of Commerce. Your local Chamber of Commerce, and Economic Development Corporation should also house this data for their annual reporting purposes.

ECONOMIC EVOLUTION

This data includes the North American Industry Classification System (NAICS) code, number of establishments, annual sales, and other data including number of employees. Individual businesses can also report to their local organizations with this information which does help in establishing Fiscal Year-end budgets to drive tourism, consumer spending and habits, as well as other relevant information necessary to design a comprehensive economic development plan.

Consumer Data can drive various campaigns, initiatives, and allocation of dollars from city, county, tribe, state and federal dollars.

Business and Industry

Business and Industry data can also be pulled from your local chamber of commerce, United States Census Bureau, and Dataus.io are all excellent sources of data. These resources are absolutely free and can help you

ECONOMIC EVOLUTION

gain an invaluable perspective to the business and industry data.

[Data Snapshot of Sawyer County, Wisconsin - Lac Courte Oreilles boundaries] In Sawyer County, specifically the Lac Courte Oreilles reservation reports the median household income as $26,827, which comes out to $12.89 per hour on full-time employment. Meanwhile, the median rent for Sawyer County is $648 per month (not including utilities), and $984 with basic utilities included. If you require child care, that's a $500/mo expense, leaving families with just $192.69 per month to pay for auto loans, auto insurance, fuel, and food to feed families.

As you can see, the tools can be highly beneficial to generate reliable data in determining a sound economic development strategy to improve the quality of life for the residents in your tribal communities.

Other data shows the Industry and Businesses which provide employment

ECONOMIC EVOLUTION

data, employment statuses, and median wages for particular employment opportunities.

Geographic Data

Geographic Data provides an in-depth look at the services and utilities which impact the quality of life. This can include transportation needs, access to broadband, fuel costs, and many other services as it relates to industry and businesses.

The geographic data can be helpful in determining the population, distance between major shopping areas for food, clothing, and essentials. Employment can be subject to transportation. Health and Human Services programs can see variables in service delivery based on your geographic area.

ECONOMIC EVOLUTION

This data will be helpful in determining proper programs and services the community needs, and which factors may play a role in the delivery of those services.

Housing Data

Housing data is important in determining property values, debt-to-earnings ratios, rents, and access to home ownership. Which areas have the majority of your low-income housing units, control rents, subsidized housing, and so on.

Other important data includes:
 Housing Affordability
 Housing Patterns
 Housing Vacancies
 New Housing (Construction)

ECONOMIC EVOLUTION

Rental Housing

Residential Financing

Education Data

Education data is an important subset of data as it relates to workforce development initiatives. While determining a quality workforce and the gap between unemployment and underemployment are directly proportionate for the majority of industry and business specific types of employment.

Let's say a manufacturing facility opens their doors in your community, do you have the capacity to fill those jobs with local individuals and contractors?

As tribal communities continually hire outside of their community, there

ECONOMIC EVOLUTION

are factors that drive these decisions. Whether we are looking at casino management, tribal leadership, program managers or enterprise managers - do our tribal members have the capacity to fill these positions without over-exhausting our training budgets?

Do the tribal programs, administrations and enterprises have to hire and train, or can they simply hire qualified individuals?

Our enterprise budgets can see a dramatic difference in hiring qualified individuals who are competent and experienced versus hiring someone with a degree and having to train them in over the course of the next six (6) to nine (9) months.

Conclusion

As this was more of a dry blog post, this is necessary information required

ECONOMIC EVOLUTION

to build out a comprehensive economic development plan for tribal communities based on reliable data.

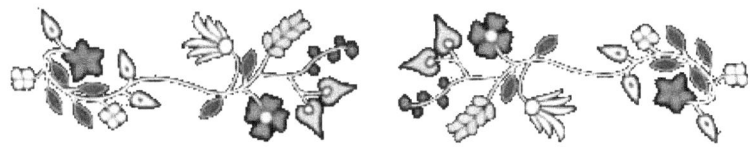

ECONOMIC EVOLUTION

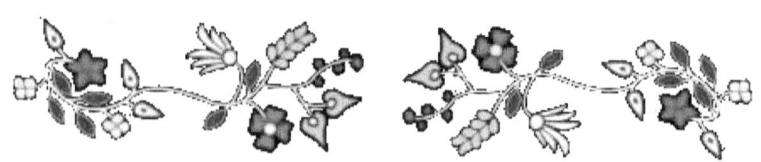

ECONOMIC EVOLUTION

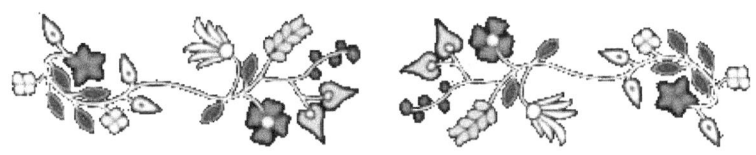

CHAPTER 10
RELEVANT EDUCATION

ECONOMIC EVOLUTION

PILLAR 2: RELEVANT EDUCATION

When we look at the educational opportunities afforded to us in our tribal communities, most of us aren't blessed enough to have a tribal colleges and universities (TCU's). These institutions are great as they can provide a great career pathways incorporating school-to-work type of partnerships, whereas local tribal enterprises can obtain training, certifications and specialized degrees that provide the local tribal enterprises with a highly qualified workforce.

ECONOMIC EVOLUTION

Unfortunately, most TCU's aren't engaged wholly with the tribal economic community. The TCU's prove 2+2 programs to bridge the students with an educational pathway to obtain an Associates degree and afford them a streamlined path to a Bachelor and Master's degree programs. These are great! This still leaves a gap with the qualified workforce.

2+2 Programs

Simply put, a 2+2 program is attending a community college for two years, then transferring to a college or university for another two years. In just four total years, a student can earn both an associate's degree and a bachelor's.

2+2 Programs are great for anyone looking to go into a specialized field of study. This educational track typically includes Registered Nurses, Certified Public Accountants, Attorneys, Information Technology,

ECONOMIC EVOLUTION

Engineers, Financial Advisor, Dentists, Plumbers, and so on. These particular career paths require a specialized training.

These programs are cost effective, close to home, knock out the general education requirements allowing the student to focus on major oriented classes once they enter University.

Skilled Trades and Specialized Programs

Skilled trades and specialized programs should be created to train, certify and license local tribal members that feed directly into the tribal enterprises as it relates to the tribal economic development plan.

When looking at the data from Pillar One: Reliable Data for Sustainable Tribal Economic Development, you'll be able to identify which areas need the most attention for workforce development.

ECONOMIC EVOLUTION

Let's say your tribe has created a construction company to focus on obtaining contracts and bids from tribal building projects. You'll need masons, carpenters, heavy equipment operators, drivers with CDL's, electricians, HVAC specialists, and plumbers. These are all skilled trades necessary to ensure you're hiring a tribal workforce that is both skilled and competent.

Apprenticeships and Internships

There are multiple resources available to individuals, communities and enterprises. The majority of internships are sponsored through your local community colleges, high schools, job centers or workforce development centers. There are vocational programs that also sponsor internships to help their participants gain valuable work experience, build up a resume, and develop connections within the local business community.

ECONOMIC EVOLUTION

Apprenticeships are very much difficult to develop as opposed to internships. Internships are paid for by the organizations, and the employer gets a free employee for a short period of time. I used to set these up all over the city of Milwaukee, Wisconsin. We built out 3 homes with a home builder using my pool of skilled tradesman looking for relevant experience while providing assistance to the local business community. Back to apprenticeships. These are typically set up with a consortium of local businesses willing to personalize a training program for an apprentice.

There are tremendous opportunities available through apprenticeships. This includes on-the-job training, one-on-one instruction, relevant experience in the latest industry trends while develop a competence level required by local employers.

ECONOMIC EVOLUTION

In my opinion, organizations like your local community college work-based learning program, Temporary Assistance for Needy Families (TANF), Vocational Rehabilitation, Job Center, Workforce Development, and local school are all great resources to develop strategic alliances to sponsor participants/students in these programs with your local business community. Once sponsored, students are obtaining direct and hands-on training from an industry professional on a local level, develop a competent and experienced, next-generation, of skilled tradesmen and women.

Example

Let me provide an example. There are community colleges that focus on transportation or construction trades, but have no pathway to direct placement upon completion. This is the simplest and most cost effective form of recruitment, hiring, and managing as most participants likely

ECONOMIC EVOLUTION

already completed an internship or work-based-learning opportunity with these enterprises.

We are addressing the challenges of; high employee turnover, unqualified workforce, training expenses, and ramp up time to bring new hires up to speed.

A great example is the Lac Courte Oreilles Ojibwa Community College with their Early Childhood Development program, which addresses all of the certifying, practicum hours, licensing, and experience needs, as well as the cultural sensitivity training needed to ensure the new hire is experienced working with culture, language, and family or community dynamics. This program pours new graduates directly into one of four (4) early-childhood development centers in the Lac Courte Oreilles community.

This can also work for construction trades, financial services, gaming.

ECONOMIC EVOLUTION

ECONOMIC EVOLUTION

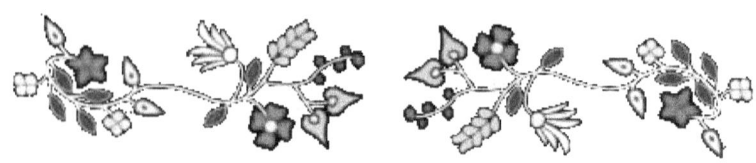

CHAPTER 11
REAL OPPORTUNITY

ECONOMIC EVOLUTION

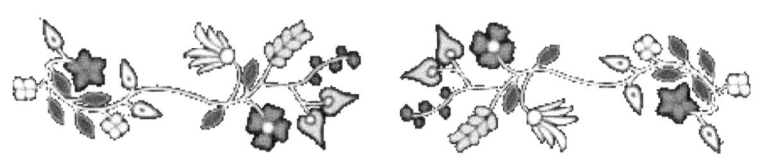

ECONOMIC EVOLUTION

PILLAR 3: REAL OPPORTUNITY

As a Native entrepreneur, I personally see the whole landscape of sustainable tribal economic development moving in the direction of tribal entrepreneurship. In order to provide real opportunities for tribal entrepreneurs, we must engage in a series of processes and initiatives that supports and empowers tribal entrepreneurs.

We have tribal preference for our hiring practices within tribal organizations and enterprises, but rarely do we have a process or policy that states you should consider tribal entrepreneurs first priority the bid on a contract or outsourced service.

The Statistics

According to a study by the United States Census Bureau, 76.2% of

ECONOMIC EVOLUTION

businesses do not have paid employees. In fact, these enterprises are small businesses which receive outsourced work or subcontracted work from other businesses. The future of sustainable economic development for tribal communities includes leveraging the tribal entrepreneurs. Tribal entrepreneurs include solopreneurs providing products, services, and solutions directly to tribal enterprises or local businesses.

In order to help foster the future of tribal entrepreneurship, we need to look at providing real opportunities for entrepreneurial spirited.

Let's look at some of the areas 'Real Opportunity' can be present.

Funding Sources

Let me be very clear, here. There are banks, credit unions, angel investors, and other forms of traditional funding which service entrepreneurs. I'm

ECONOMIC EVOLUTION

talking about leveraging alternative funding sources available to areas with disadvantaged populations.

Native CDFI (Community Development Financial Institutions) is a great resource for tribal members. Most of the Native CDFI's have multiple programs which they can engage their target audience, tribal members. CDFI's really shine in helping individuals who are under-banked or un-bankable. The CDFI can posture as the bridge between a traditional bank or credit union, where they are unable to offer them traditional services due to poor credit, negative marks on their credit report, no credit, or bad debt.

Native CDFI's also offer business loans to tribal entrepreneurs. If you're an entrepreneur and seeking out resources to grow, expand or develop your business, look to Native CDFI's. In Wisconsin, we have First Nations Community Financial, Niijii Capital Partners, Wisconsin Indian Loan Fund,

ECONOMIC EVOLUTION

and First American Community Capital.

Another resource are Community Development Loan Funds (CDFL's). These are great resources to help community members gain access to capital.

Business Incubator

Business Incubators provide training, resources, office space, networking and critical business connections through the resources within the business incubator. Also known as a, "Business Accelerator", the idea is to leverage a locally owned organization such as an Economic Development Corporation with access to county, city, state, and federal dollars providing shared resources to its members of the incubator. Coworking spaces provide excellent opportunities to small businesses and start-ups, enabling the power of networking and resource sharing for your projects, services or collaborative works. A business accelerator or incubator allow

ECONOMIC EVOLUTION

you access to the mentoring, training, and other resources available through the economic development corporation.

Entrepreneurial Training

In the early stages of an entrepreneurial endeavor, most entrepreneur's pinpoint their challenges to the ramp-up portion of their business to:

+ Access to Capital

+ Access to Mentoring

+ Access to Networks/Key Players

+ Access to Qualified Employees/Subcontractors

+ Access to Affordable and Relevant Training

While the incubator and accelerator offer the majority of these challenges, the last one is associated with training which is both affordable and relevant to their business.

ECONOMIC EVOLUTION

Local community colleges offer classes, however the classes are generally process oriented, versus relevant to the business owner. Let's use the example of bookkeeping and accounting processes. If you're needing to set up a ledger of accounts for vendors, partners, board members and employees to be compensated. The class may not address these specific needs - hence, "Relevant Education."

Government Contracting

Lastly, there are tremendous opportunities associated with bidding on government contracts. Whether you're leveraging the power of an 8(a) designation from the SBA (Small Business Administration) or the HubZone designation, the majority of government contracts do require you to have one of many designations to bid on these contracts. SAM, the system for award management, is a Federal Government owned and operated free

ECONOMIC EVOLUTION

web site that consolidates the capabilities in Central Contractor Registration (CCR)/FedReg, Online Representations and Certifications Application (ORCA) and the Excluded Parties List System (EPLS).

This resource allows you to seek out local bids for government contracts.

The lowest hanging fruit is to bid on cleaning contracts. Yes, cleaning contracts. Local government buildings like the local court house, corrections office, low-income housing units, or forestry and FDA properties. There are also research facilities and military offices which allow bidding for cleaning services to local entrepreneurs eligible through the SAM system.

Other considerations include FEMA disaster recovery projects, mining, transportation, and department of commerce.

ECONOMIC EVOLUTION

Procurement Policy

All of this starts and ends with a quality procurement process to vet all local entrepreneurs to subcontract out the work to local entrepreneurs. A tribal government can bid on the contracts, win the bids and outsource the work to local tribal entrepreneurs. The money stays in the community, and the tribe continually wins government contracts. Did I mention the money stays in the community?

If a tribal procurement process empowering tribal entrepreneurs were available there would be greater opportunities for tribal entrepreneurs to engage within their own community, service their local tribal enterprises, and employ members of their community.

Here is an example of how this would work. As a tribal entrepreneur, I approach tribal leaders and business development corporations often in

ECONOMIC EVOLUTION

regards to proposing my products, services and solutions. My own tribe has saved tremendous amounts of money by utilizing my services and I turn around and purchase gas, eat at the restaurants, and shop at their retail locations.

The money stays in the community.

Every tribe has skilled tradesman in the areas of landscaping, carpentry, masonry, electrical, mechanics, heavy equipment operators and commercial driver's license holders - and so on. These entrepreneurs can bid on contracts with the tribal health center, casino, convenience stores, and any other asset properties the tribe owns. Again, the money stays in the community, we are supporting tribal entrepreneurs and through the incubators empowering members through capacity building, and training opportunities.

ECONOMIC EVOLUTION

To take this a step further, the tribal organizations with 8(a) or HubZone certified enterprises can subcontract to these entrepreneurs, save massive amounts of money on payroll liabilities, insurance, and managerial oversight, while satisfying the federal requirements of minority workforce.

I hope that has been helpful in understanding how to garner development strategies for creating real opportunity for local tribal entrepreneurs.

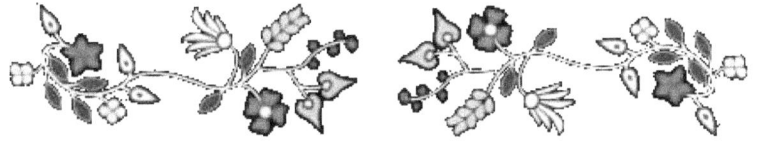

ECONOMIC EVOLUTION

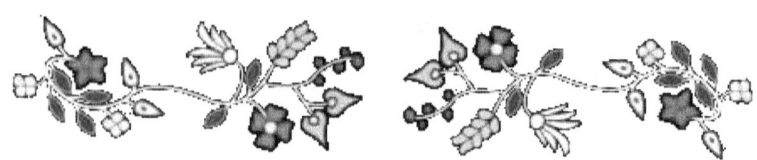

ECONOMIC EVOLUTION

 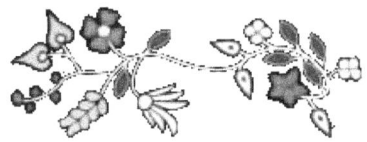

CHAPTER 12
MOBILE TECHNOLOGY and INNOVATIONS

ECONOMIC EVOLUTION

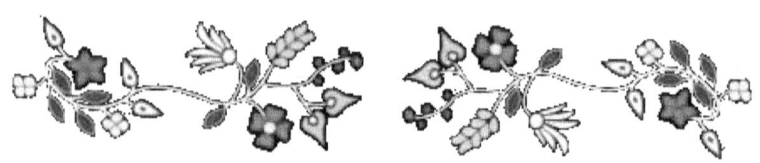

ECONOMIC EVOLUTION

PILLAR 4: MOBILE TECHNOLOGY

Technology has leveled the playing field for any business, provided these businesses are leveraging the power of technology. I personally know two to three dozen digital entrepreneurs that have built 6-figure businesses from their kitchen table while leveraging the power of social media platforms. In their pajamas, they can create aggressive marketing campaigns to help businesses generate more qualified leads, quotes, and clients through free platforms like Facebook, YouTube, Google, Instagram, Snapchat, Twitter and many others.

In addition to digital entrepreneurs, mobile technology can benefit premisc-based enterprises, much like we have on tribal lands, with online ordering, e-commerce and digital products. We can generate and approve loan applications from people from all over the United States we have never met, nor will we ever meet. Within 24 hours, we lend short-term

ECONOMIC EVOLUTION

loans and can generate millions in revenue through this mobile technology.

Let's look at five (5) ways to leverage the power of mobile technologies for sustainable tribal economic development.

1. Direct Job Creation

One of the and largest and most used services include, "Virtual Assistants." Personally, I leverage the power of mobile technology by hiring six (6) sub-contractors throughout the world. I have tribal members, individuals from India, Pakistan, Philippines, and Mexico. These individuals work remotely from the comfort of their home and provide a valuable service directly to a small business in Hayward, Wisconsin. Every tribe can leverage Virtual Assistants from anywhere, using the same criteria for hiring, and allow employment opportunities on part-time,

ECONOMIC EVOLUTION

on-call or full-time employment. If you're in Florida and wish to hire tribal members from California, Washington or South Dakota, mobile technology makes this possible, and your local job market can no longer be an issue with under qualified individuals. Obviously, as you move further up the administrative hierarchy, you'll require more face-to-face, on-site time with the leadership team and organization.

2. Reduced Costs

The majority of organizations, companies and enterprises can leverage the power of mobile technology by outsourcing tedious and repetitive tasks. It has been said that upper-level management employees spend an average of 47 hours per month doing repetitive tasks outside of the normal scope of their job. Now, when you hire for that managerial position, you're more than likely seeking management of the organizations resources, operations, policies, and procedures to ensure they're getting met and

ECONOMIC EVOLUTION

exceeding that of the established requirements. By leveraging sub-contracted remote employees, you reduce your payroll liabilities, office space, insurance, and on-site management.

3. New Services and Industries

The emergence of new service and industries can be 100% attributed to mobile technologies. One of the industries that come to mind include, "Online Courses." Sparkki, a platform specializing in online courses provide multi-platform courses, training, and on-boarding functions allowing your employees to be hired, trained, and tested on competency without them stepping foot into an office. Additional considerations include, training entrepreneurs and business owners on critical business functions; accounting, marketing, sales, management styles, programming, information technology and other integral services necessary for flourishing enterprises.

ECONOMIC EVOLUTION

Take the example of online lending. This is a new industry for tribes to engage. Tribes can lend money to people using mobile technology, which includes all of the components of lead generation, application submissions, underwriting, automated clearing house transfers, and loan management. Most tribes engage on the collections level as an initial phase and progress into other areas of the business, including but not limited to; calling delinquent accounts, processing collection payments, compliance, and underwriting.

4. Workforce Transformation

New "microwork" platforms, developed by companies like Upwork, Freelancer, Amazon and FreeUp, help to divide tasks into small components that can then be outsourced to contract workers. The contractors are often based in emerging economies. Microwork platforms

ECONOMIC EVOLUTION

allow entrepreneurs to significantly cut costs and get access to qualified workers. In 2017, Upwork alone had over 3 million registered contractors who performed 1.5 million tasks. This trend had spillover effects on other industries, such as online payment systems. Microwork has also contributed to the rise of entrepreneurship, making it much easier for self-starters to access best practices, legal and regulatory information, marketing and investment resources.

According to the United States Census Bureau, 76.2% of registered businesses in the United States do not have paid employees. This is attributing to the fact that the workforce is transforming and moving to entrepreneurship and work-from-home opportunities. The majority of these small businesses are operating in the "Business Process Outsourcing" (BPO) sector. They find businesses that have repetitive tasks, monotonous tasks, tedious tasks, on up to high-level tasks to be outsourced and secure contracts with those organizations and enterprises.

ECONOMIC EVOLUTION

Personally, I worked with six (6) tribes in the Midwest through BPO contracts. Tribes contract me to provide specific tasks related to marketing and business development.

5. Business Innovations

In the United States, more than 95% of businesses have an online presence. The Internet provides them with new ways of reaching out to customers and competing for market share. Over the past few years, social media has established itself as a powerful marketing tool. Information and communication tools employed within companies help to streamline business processes and improve efficiency. The unprecedented explosion of connected devices throughout the world has created new ways for businesses to serve their customers.

Whether you're looking at implementing online applications, leveraging

ECONOMIC EVOLUTION

application programming interface (API) technology to incorporate electronic signatures, and search engines to attract customers. Mobile technology has contributed to this improvement in efficiency and explosion of customer base. There are no longer borders limiting revenue potential, the internet allows a level playing field with anyone seeking leverage the power of mobile technology.

Examples of Mobile Technologies

Other considerations include training and technical assistance through mobile technology. I have been involved with Community Development Financial Institutions since 2010 and realized there were some geo-based challenges associated with supporting tribal entrepreneurship. Many of the participants seeking to start a small business had to arrive at the office, take a 60 minute class in financial management, marketing, management, budgeting, and so on. The biggest challenge these

ECONOMIC EVOLUTION

participants experienced was associated with transportation, specifically in rural areas. Mobile technology can solve that. An online business training and technical assistance module can train in program participants in all areas of business ownership, while allowing the Native CDFI organization full transparency to the reporting functions of their progress. These are progress reports can be part of their development plan for the next round of funds released for the aspiring tribal entrepreneur.

My Personal Development Journey using Mobile Technology

Personally, I took three (3) online courses to help me develop an entirely new service which produces ⅓ of my annual revenue. These courses were $299 each and I have made that back on my first 4 clients. New client acquisition can be done from the comfort of my home, in my pajamas, updates and maintenance are completed from my laptop or mobile device.

ECONOMIC EVOLUTION

Remote services are what I'm talking about here. Mobile technology allows Remote Services to be a critical service most companies tend to hire for - they can now outsource that to businesses like me and many other virtual entrepreneurs.

Conclusion

The most efficient and effective approach to leverage and monetize mobile technologies is to look at current market trends. What are people looking to achieve, accomplish and secure through online platforms? Is it diet and exercise, is it funding and capital, is it online education, or is it a unique shopping experience? Whatever you're ideal clients are seeking, find that need and fill it with a product, service or solution you're able to deliver on a mobile technology platform.

ECONOMIC EVOLUTION

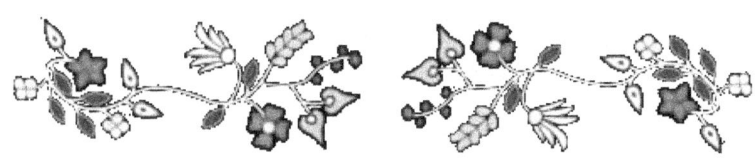

ECONOMIC EVOLUTION

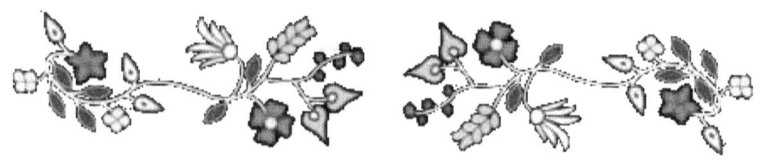

CHAPTER 13
YOUTH ENGAGEMENT

ECONOMIC EVOLUTION

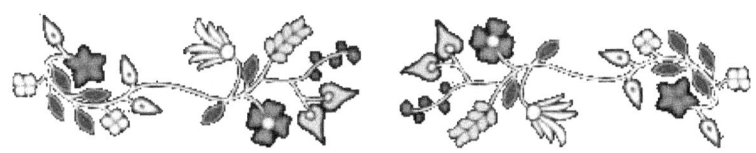

ECONOMIC EVOLUTION

PILLAR 5: YOUTH ENGAGEMENT

This is the final pillar, only because I personally find it the most crucial component. I'm a strong advocate for youth development, specifically tribal youth development. My younger years included becoming a three sport athlete, and going on to play basketball at the collegiate level. The character developed includes aspects of leadership, team-building, self-improvement, and taking direction for the greater good of the group or team. These are characteristics most hiring managers and recruiters are looking for.

This process should start early, and here is why. As a Native tribal youth continues on with their younger years and advance into high school, they begin to craft their vision for their future. There are two boats they can take post-graduation.

ECONOMIC EVOLUTION

Boat number one includes, going off to the university of their choice, obtaining a bachelor's, master's or doctorate degree in one specialization - only to return and help improve their own community, become a leader, if you will. Boat number two includes, working in one of the local tribal enterprises, climbing the corporate ladder, and helping improve their community internally.

The internal conversation that goes on with the youth revolves around, "How can I participate, and do I want to participate?"

I'm going to share with you five (5) ways youth can transform the economic landscape of our tribal communities.

1. **Labor Force**

Once the youth of our community become of working age, they're now a

ECONOMIC EVOLUTION

critical part of our local labor force. Keep in mind, when the youth do engage in local employment, they're very observant. They can see when a manager isn't on-site or vaguely present in the enterprise or organization. They observe the culture of the workplace, the treatment employees garner from leadership and management. Most importantly, they're learning what it is like for the future years to come, as an young-adult. Is this something they want to be a part of? Is this an enterprise they want to grow with? Is this a community they want to be a part of?

2. Consumers

Youth are very good consumers. They purchase the latest goods and services trending in the social realms of their world. A portion of their income goes to the state in which they reside, helping them realize the importance of consumerism through paying taxes. Where are their tax dollars going? Are they going to online shopping platforms like eBay,

ECONOMIC EVOLUTION

Amazon, and Google Shopping? Do those dollars stay within the community in which they reside? These trends will drive demand generation for products, services and solutions. There are simple facts associated with the youth of our communities.

Every youth will use a mobile device to purchase apps, communicate with friends, and use a form of transportation. This means, they will buy a phone, purchase a data plan, use local transportation or purchase a vehicle, and seek out entertainment venues. Are these present in your local marketplace? If not, those dollars will leave the community.

3. Entrepreneurs

Youth love the increasing levels of independence. As they increase the young-adult ages, they look to valid careers, and this can include entrepreneurship. Are they gaining valuable experience from their local

ECONOMIC EVOLUTION

employers to help gain skills, experience and competencies allowing them to engage in entrepreneurship within their own community. In some tribal communities, you'll find lawn care businesses, painting businesses, auto detailing, and social media management services, among other internet marketing-based companies.

After all, the younger generations spend more time on social platforms than most adults. This allows a tremendous leg-up on prior generations whom may not have been so involved with these social media platforms or internet marketing platforms.

One prediction I will make is that the youth of our communities will be the technologically advanced generations for years to come. This will include businesses processes, mobile application development, technology integrations, mobile device uses and optimization, as well as social media and internet marketing platform extraction for new client generation.

ECONOMIC EVOLUTION

Whether we are looking to leverage Snapchat, Facebook, Instagram, Twitter, Pinterest, YouTube, Tumblr, Marco Polo, WhatsApp, Telegram and WeChat - to name a few. These mobile applications can play an integral part in the lead generation process to reach prospective clients on a more personal level, allowing for a unique buying experience. Mobile apps allow for greater targeting, and personalization of marketing messages that reach individuals on these platforms.

4. Agents for Change

The youth of our community can be massively beneficial to the change that is required within our communities. We are seeing this happen now in the schools, universities, and social circles. The days of 9-5, 8-hour, work days are becoming less common. We are seeing coworking and collaborative work spaces where remote employees can work from virtual locations and contribute to the company, organization or enterprise

ECONOMIC EVOLUTION

without ever stepping foot into the office.

The two forms of change can occur with the two boats we mentioned above. The youth can decide to leave the community, acquire advanced degrees in an area of specialization; accounting, law, finance, technology, programming, healthcare, language, culture or historical preservation. They bring these teachings back to the community for improving upon the current state of the community, economy and workforce.

The other boat allows the youth stay in the community, generate valuable work skills and focus on improving the state of the community in real-time. These youth will work their way up the corporate hierarchy, so to speak, learn the intricacies of the political landscape as it relates to tribal employment, education, culture, language, and quality of life for themselves and their peers. These are the leaders of our communities with hands-on experience and climbed the leadership ladder from within.

ECONOMIC EVOLUTION

Either boat provides a pathway to become an agent for change within our very own tribal communities.

5. Civic Engagement

Civic Engagement allows youth to get involved from various levels of the community ranging from health and human services, to youth development, and economic development initiatives. We look at organizations like The Boy's & Girls Club in Indian Country, social programs, culture camps, language immersion camps and other mentor-oriented civic organizations allowing youth to play in a mentor capacity and help others in their shoes.

Some of the best programs to promote civic engagement are to include the youth in these vital roles to address some of the most prominent

ECONOMIC EVOLUTION

challenges in Indian Country. Whether we are addressing housing, healthcare, drug abuse, alcoholism, single parent homes, or addressing poverty and homelessness. We allow our youth to see what it is like to experience these situations from the lens of a program advocate, community member, peer, and future leader of their community.

They get first-hand experience in observing, and addressing the challenges plaguing the community. Other benefits for youth involved in civic engagement get additional points on their college applications increasing probability for admission and acceptance.

Conclusion

The youth are the future, it has been said time and time again. The fact remains, youth can only go one direction, and that is up. We must produce programs, services, and create real opportunities for our youth engage and

ECONOMIC EVOLUTION

learn how to become critical and productive members of our communities. The best thing we could do for our children is allow them to partake in tremendous opportunities from sports, civic clubs, culture, language, business, arts and music to create well-rounded young-adults providing our communities with the most functional generations ever to become our leaders. Innovations, technology, and experienced youth can only be of benefit to our tribal communities and their on quality of life.

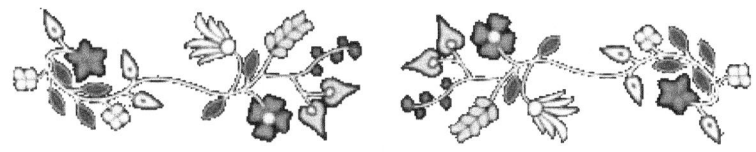

ECONOMIC EVOLUTION

ECONOMIC EVOLUTION

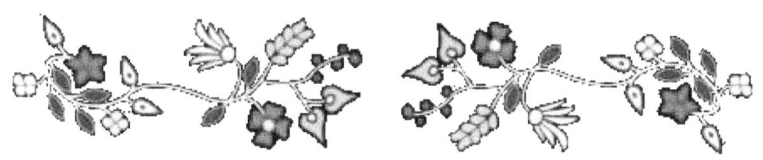

CHAPTER 14
EMPOWER DEVELOP PROSPER

ECONOMIC EVOLUTION

ECONOMIC EVOLUTION

EMPOWER. DEVELOP. PROSPER

This is a theory of mine, I have began to explore in 2016 when I was running for my community's Tribal Governing Board, and hoping to obtain a seat and focus on economic development.

I began mapping out various models which included people. People of the community, and people of the surrounding communities.

The primary goal was to create a model which empowered individuals within a given community. This process begins with a question. That question is, "How can we get involved?" It just so happens, that we can get involved on various levels, provided you have the passion, ambition and mindset to be an agent of change. I realize we hear that all the time, "Be an agent of change" or "Be the change you want to see." These aren't just phrases or sayings, they are statements those who fully believe they can

ECONOMIC EVOLUTION

inspire change within their own communities are saying. They are not just saying them, they are believing in them.

EMPOWER

While we begin to get involved, we want to identify which area we want to make an impact. If it is Data, we can conduct community-wide surveys and collect reliable data to help in the decision making process for organizations. If it is Education, we can join board and committees on the local level with head start programs, elementary schools, middle schools, high schools, and college or vocational schools. It is very wise for these institutions to form committees and boards allowing parents and community members to be involved with their local schools and educational institutions. If we are talking about opportunity, we can join business boards, attend economic development corporation meetings, or chamber of commerce events, and so on. On the technology and

ECONOMIC EVOLUTION

innovations side, we can get involved with various projects focused on leveraging technology and innovations to improve upon the infrastructure of our local communities. Every community has a large volume of participation in youth sports, youth programs and youth initiatives.

The organizations are eagerly seeking individuals to join in on the discussion, provide real life data from those who are participating. While it is great to run reports and paint a picture. Participants will have the best data from within the organization, itself.

The goal with this model is to Empower the people of the community to get involved in shaping the opportunities for our youth, community members and elderly. It is very common for an agency to pull data and say, "We need a program for _____" and disregard the feedback from community members who live, work and play in these communities. This

ECONOMIC EVOLUTION

type of ready, aim, aim, aim, aim, and fire type of approach, all to often, misses the mark on solving the challenges within the community.

DEVELOP

When we look at this model, we are allowing the organizational executives to determine the direction of our community without the feedback of our members. When we lean on the people, we now are attacking challenges from within. This is the empowerment portion of the EMPOWER. DEVELOP. PROSPER model.

Now, once we deploy these resources and allow members, parents, children, and elderly in our communities to reside on these committees and boards, we are exploring capacity building. Allowing the people to drive the initiatives, goals, mission and results of initiative. Committees are seeing both; development of capacity, skill sets, and competence, as

ECONOMIC EVOLUTION

well as resource ownership. The development of this type of mindset is powerful for the community as a whole, its members, and the leadership of elected officials.

PROSPER

Once these groups of individuals start seeing results from their efforts, commitment, and diligence, we create an environment of prosperity. The people can become the change they wanted to see, they become leaders in their community, regardless of title, regardless of elected or in a volunteer capacity.

This type of prosperity is from within, the members of the community can see they are agents of change, and can make an impact. There is a saying that goes something like this, "A Chain is As Strong As The Weakest Link", and when we strengthen all of our links, we have one strong chain.

ECONOMIC EVOLUTION

That chain comes in the form of our local economy, local community, and local individuals.

The Old Strategy

Gone are the days of finding the best and brightest, sending them off to prestigious institutions, only to hope, wish and pray they return to the community to come back and solve all of the problems. This creates a corporate hierarchy and assumption of power with someone who isn't attached to the community, as they were gone for the last four (4) to eight (8) years. People are skeptical, and they should be. They don't trust the individual with the advanced degree and assume they know every intricacy of the community and how the dynamics work to form a comprehensive economic development strategy.

ECONOMIC EVOLUTION

The New Strategy

Build from within. If you're improving upon your grocery store, leveraging the power of those who shop at that grocery store. What do they love about shopping there? Is it the product, price, proximity, people, or some other intangible we cannot see on the surface level?

Build from within. If you're improving upon your schools, leverage the power of those who send their children to your school. What do they love about attending your school? Is it the curriculum, teachers, administration, athletics and extracurricular activities, proximity, or some other intangible we are unaware of? The best approach is to ask those students, teachers and staff what makes your school great and exploit those strengths while minimizing weaknesses.

ECONOMIC EVOLUTION

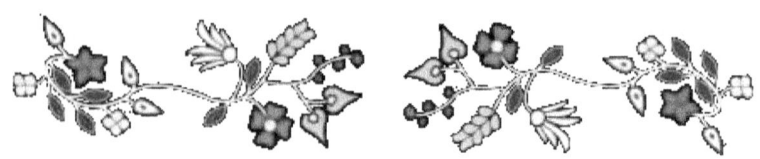

ECONOMIC EVOLUTION

CHAPTER 15
CONCLUSION

ECONOMIC EVOLUTION

ECONOMIC EVOLUTION

CONCLUSION

I truly hope each and every one of you had learned at least one thing you can apply to your local economic development efforts.

Whether we are adding new elements to focus on one of the pillars, or utilizing the entire Structural Equilibrium theory to build out a sustainable and well-balanced approach which grows all areas within the community from utilization of the pillars. The way I see it. We can grow our communities through three different approaches.

Pillar-Specific

The low-hanging fruit, is to pick a pillar and develop on just that until you have a succinct and clear direction of which pillar is strongest in your community. If it is data. Start with data, survey every aspect of your

ECONOMIC EVOLUTION

community to uncover any and all opportunities which are able to be developed, as well as areas with which produced to the most inefficient results, aka most wasteful.

Structural Equilibrium (Balanced-Approach)

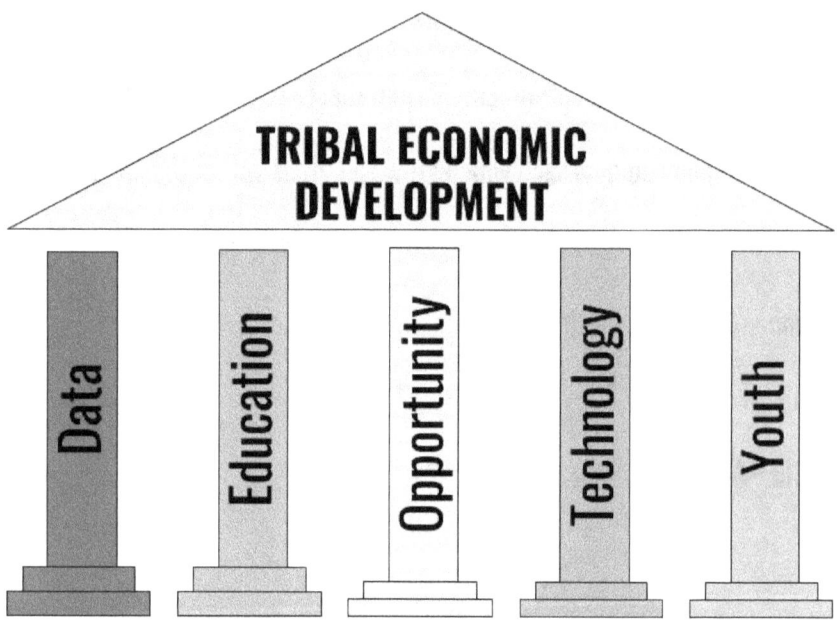

Utilize the entire spectrum of the pillars, and incorporate all resources, supports, and opportunities into one comprehensive plan which would be

ECONOMIC EVOLUTION

the Structural Equilibrium, discussed in Chapter 2. Structural Equilibrium refers to the complete structure of an economic development model. Those pillars that hold up the local economy are foundational, and those pillars are what consist of the strengths your local community can offer. The way I drew out those pillars, are heavily associated and deeply rooted into how a strong Community-Led Economic Development model can develop, grow and sustain from the inside-out, with the people as the core. Without people, we are simply operating with a subset of policies, procedure, and paperwork. We cannot build businesses with policies, procedures, and paperwork. We can steer the company in the right direction, but when people quit, you must recruit, hire, train and retain a whole new individual.

If you simply grow from within, and leverage the power of the people, your policies, procedures, and paperwork, simply drive the process for the

ECONOMIC EVOLUTION

people who are dedicated, committed to a particular mission, goal or objective.

People contain passion. I am of the school of thought, there are two types of people in this world. People who work for your money, and people who work for your passion. When people can get behind your missions, goals, and objectives - you have a recipe for success. This is where Community-Led Economic Development must begin.

These pillars include equal focus from various groups of people with the passion to bring these initiatives to life. Every community has groups of individuals passionate about youth. Every community has groups of individuals passionate about technology and innovations. Every community has groups of individuals passionate about something of importance to a pillar which strengthens and defines your economic development structure. That my friends, is Structural Equilibrium.

ECONOMIC EVOLUTION

Collaboration

Each community has groups of agencies and organizations leveraging government programs, state funds, or non-profit funds. They have their initiatives, goals and objectives. These are great agencies to partner with to bring together a comprehensive economic development model.

As an example, a neighboring town is focused on manufacturing and production. Another neighboring town is known for transportation and distribution. In these towns, there are entrepreneurs or small businesses offering advertising, marketing and sales solutions. Each town has people seeking meaningful careers, sustainable jobs and real opportunity as defined in Chapter 11.

A strong Community-Led approach is about capacity building, and using the EMPOWER. DEVELOP. PROSPER model.

ECONOMIC EVOLUTION

The goal of this book is to empower the leaders of our communities to think differently, consider the fact that people have power. People have capacity, and without people, our programs, businesses or organizations wouldn't exist.

We need people to buy our products or services, we need people to participate in our programs to continue the funding for said program, and we need people in our organizations to continue community-led initiatives serving various segments of individuals.

The goal is to allow people to get involved in the decision making process, empower them to get involved and engaged. Allow them to develop the capacity, skill sets and competence to run organizations from an organic standpoint. Once people realize they can become agents of change, now we allow them to prosper from the fruits of their labor.

ECONOMIC EVOLUTION

If an organization, business, or community succeeds and fails, it is because we failed our people. Allow people to get involved.

EMPOWER

DEVELOP

PROSPER

I invite every single one of you reading this book to look into your own organizations and identify areas where you can leverage the users, participants, and community members to get involved.

In a business scenario, you can leverage the power of shoppers. Allow shoppers to conduct research on customer experience, customer service, pricing, inventory, and so on. This report can drive the success of your

ECONOMIC EVOLUTION

business, by catering to the products and services your customer base will be most desirable. A second approach is to find out what they leave the community to acquire. If they are leaving the community to purchase shoes. Why don't we offer those shoes in our community? If they are leaving for school clothes. Why aren't we offering those trendy clothes in our community? If people are leaving for entertainment and movies. Why aren't we offering those entertainment venues in our community?

The most important facet in any business is revenue, second are expenses to produce margins, then we look into other aspects like buying habits. If we can hone in on what our community members are buying online, and from other communities - we can perceivably bring those dollars back to our community.

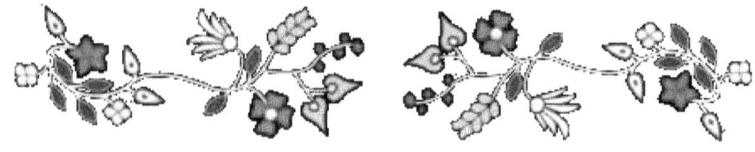

ECONOMIC EVOLUTION

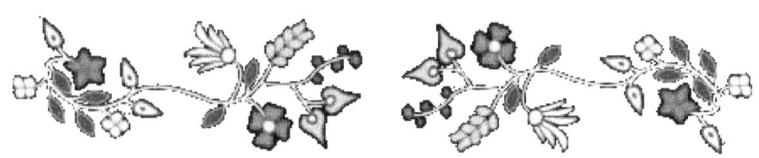